Rookie Read-About® Science

Hot and Cold

By Allan Fowler

Consultants
Robert L. Hillerich, Professor Emeritus,
Bowling Green State University, Bowling Green, Ohio;
Consultant, Pinellas County Schools, Florida

Lynne Kepler, Educational Consultant

Fay Robinson, Child Development Specialist

CHILDRENS PRESS®
CHICAGO

Design by Beth Herman Design Associates
Photo Research by Feldman & Associates, Inc.

Library of Congress Cataloging-in-Publication Data

Fowler, Allan.
    Hot and cold / by Allan Fowler.
       p. cm. –(Rookie read-about science)
    ISBN 0-516-06021-X
    1. Heat–Juvenile literature. 2. Cold–Juvenile literature.
  3. Temperature–Juvenile literature. [1. Heat. 2. Cold. 3. Temperature.]
  I. Title. II. Series.
QC256.F68 1994
536–dc20
                                   93-38588
                                        CIP
                                        AC

How hot is a hot day?

If you're sweating, it must
be pretty hot.

A swim in cold water will
cool you off.

How cold is a cold day?
If you're shivering, it must
be pretty cold.

Sitting in front of a
fireplace will warm
you up.

To say exactly how hot or cold the weather is, we use a number. This number is called the temperature.

On a warm day, the number is higher than on a cold day. You can find out the temperature by looking at a thermometer.

It feels good to stand in
the warm sun on a bright
spring day.

Most of our heat comes from the sun. Without heat from the sun, few things could grow; few things could live.

Around the North Pole
and South Pole, it is cold
all the time.

Very few kinds of plants
or animals can live where
there is so little heat.

Other places stay warm
all year around.

These places are called the tropics. They are often covered by plants and are filled with animal life.

We put heat to work for us.
We cook our food with heat.

We keep our homes
warm on cold days.

A high, or warm, temperature causes many things to expand, or grow bigger.

On bridges, a little space is left between the steel beams. This gives the beams room to expand on hot days.

Hot and cold temperatures can change the form of things. Hard metals will melt in the heat of a fire.

This soft dough becomes a
firm loaf of bread when
you bake it in a hot oven.

If you make water hot
enough, it starts to boil
and turns into steam.

When water drops to a
low enough temperature,
it freezes into ice.

A low, or cold, temperature causes many things to contract, or get smaller.

In the winter, the mercury in a thermometer contracts and shows a low temperature.

Although cold makes most things contract, some liquids expand when they freeze.

This milk expanded when it froze — and popped right out of the bottle.

A mixture of cream, milk, sugar, and flavoring becomes ice cream if it is left in a freezer.

On a warm day, you have to eat your ice cream fast. If you don't, it will melt . . . and then you will be drinking ice cream soup!

Words You Know

sweating

shivering

boil   steam

tropics

temperature   thermometer

heat   ice

31

Index

animals, 13, 15
boil, 22, 30
bread, 21
bridges, 18
cold, 6, 9, 12, 17, 24, 26
cold water, 5
cook, 16
cool, 5
contract, 24, 26
dough, 21
expand, 18, 26
fire, 20
fireplace, 7
food, 16
freeze, 23, 26
heat, 11, 13, 16, 20, 31
hot, 3, 4, 9, 18, 22
ice, 23, 31
ice cream, 29
liquids, 26

mercury, 24
metals, 20
North Pole, 12
number, 9
oven, 21
plants, 13, 15
shivering, 6, 30
South Pole, 12
steam, 22, 30
steel beams, 18
sun, 10, 11
sweating, 4, 30
swim, 5
temperature, 9, 18, 20, 23, 24, 31
thermometer, 9, 24, 31
tropics, 15, 30
warm, 7, 9, 10, 14, 17, 18
water, 22, 23
weather, 9

About the Author

Allan Fowler is a free-lance writer with a background in advertising. Born in New York, he lives in Chicago now and enjoys traveling.

Photo Credits

PhotoEdit – ©David Young-Wolff, 4, 16, 17, 30 (top left); ©Merritt A. Vincent, 7; ©Tony Freeman, 8, 11, 22, 30 (bottom left), 31 (top); ©Mark Burnett, 19

Tom Stack & Associates—©David M. Dennis, 19 (inset)

SuperStock International, Inc. – Ron Dahlquist, Cover; ©James Ong, 5; ©Tom Rosenthal, 10, 25; ©Peter Van Rhijn, 14, 30 (bottom right); ©Prim and Ray Manley, 20, 31 (bottom left); ©George Jacobs, 23, 31 (bottom right)

Tony Stone Images— ©Ken Griffiths, 12; ©Bryn Campbell, 13

Valan – ©Robert C. Simpson, 6, 30 (top right); ©John Cancalosi, 15; ©Kennon Cooke, 21; ©A.B. Joyce, 27; ©V. Wilkinson, 28

COVER: Girls eating ice cream